"What a wonderful lit~~ ___ ~~ Quinn's insightful and tical reflections will speak to the heart of every parent."

FR. JAMES MALLON, *Pastor and Author of Divine Renovation: Moving Your Parish from Maintenance to Mission*

"*At Home in the Heart of God* provides encouragement for parents who are rediscovering the Catholic faith in their own lives and learning how to share it with their children."

JOHN ROBERTO, *Author of Lifelong Faith: Formation for All Ages and Generations*

"There is so much packed into this easy-to-read booklet. The very building blocks of our Catholic faith are here, presented in a way that never felt over my head."

TINA, *Mom*

"The message is powerful...that the perceived gap between the sacred and the everyday of family living is not nearly as wide as we tend to think."

LEIF KEHRWALD, *National Speaker, Author, and Pastoral Minister, St. Charles Parish, Portland, OR*

"A must-read for parents who seek heaven for themselves and their kids."

CARLOS, *Dad*

"A great booklet for parents, full of encouragement, story, and meaningful teaching. This welcoming, "come as you are" booklet connects the importance of learning to walk with the eucharistic Lord and being the parent you want to be. I warmly recommend it as a meaningful, and even life-changing, gift for parents bringing children to the Church to receive Baptism or First Communion."

SUSAN WINDLEY-DAOUST, *Director of Missionary Discipleship, Diocese of Winona-Rochester*

"If you're a parent who struggles to get your family to church, or even understand why you should want to, then *At Home in the Heart of God* was written just for you."

FR. PJ MCMANUS, *Pastor, Christ the King Parish, Des Moines, Iowa*

"I'd like to put this marvelous, touching book into the hands of every Catholic parent!"

BILL HUEBSCH, *Author of Promise and Hope: Pastoral Theology in the Age of Mercy*

"This is authentic to who Tom Quinlan is, expressing his love for God, his family, his Catholic faith, and the Eucharist."

DENISE UTTER, *Author of Engage Every Family: A Parish Guide to Integrated Faith*

AT HOME IN THE HEART OF GOD

At Home
IN THE
Heart
OF
God

FAMILY, JESUS,
AND THE **EUCHARIST**

TOM QUINLAN

TWENTY-THIRD
PUBLICATIONS
twentythirdpublications.com

TWENTY-THIRD PUBLICATIONS
977 Hartford Turnpike Unit A
Waterford, CT 06385
(860) 437-3012 or (800) 321-0411
www.twentythirdpublications.com

Cover photos: stock.adobe.com

ISBN: 978-1-62785-787-1
Printed in the U.S.A.

 A division of Bayard, Inc.

CONTENTS

INTRODUCTION

I AM A CATHOLIC AND A PARENT. That means I believe that Jesus is God. And that I never get to watch a ballgame uninterrupted. Or have the house clean for very long. Being a parent means pouring yourself out in love *constantly*.

This short book tries to show the connection between your love as a mom or dad and God's love for us. As Catholic Christians, we see Jesus as the proof of just how intensely God loves us. We recognize this particularly in Jesus' journey through suffering and death to Resurrection and the gift he left us at the Last Supper, the Eucharist.

I will share some practical insights from my journey of life, family, and faith. And together, we'll consider the transformative *good news* that Jesus offers us.

Whatever your level of engagement with Catholic faith (including none), I hope this book will make you smile and think and reflect with gratitude. And maybe explore how a eucharistic lifestyle can be a blessing to you, your parenthood, and your family.

Turn to the next page to read more about the special place you have in God's heart...a heart that desires to feed us with the Eucharist for the journey ahead as adults and as parents.

Parenthood

Generosity and Meaning

WILL IT MATTER 100 YEARS FROM NOW?

Much of what we do in our lives won't. Heck, a lot won't matter in five months. But here's one thing I guarantee will matter in 100 years: *parenting.*

In fact, every little thing we do to love and care for our children and help them become their full selves will echo forward, rippling out for all eternity! No pressure now, moms and dads, eh?

As someone who is married with two little boys, I can see it. How every day, Danny and Matt are learning and changing. They are watching Kristi and me and picking up ideas and behaviors from us all the time. These are hugely impactful, formative years. Our boys are becoming, moment to moment, who they will be as adults. If they have children, our parenting now will impact their descendants and the course of history. Even if they don't have children, who they are will make the world a better (or worse) place forever.

Parenting is so meaningful and rewarding. And so exhausting! We continually give without asking the cost. It is a lesson in generosity and humility. Parenting stretches us and teaches us how to be adults ourselves!

Parents are the unsung heroes of society. Videos of you cleaning the kitchen will never go viral. No awards are given for bathing your little one or patiently helping with your kids' homework. The sacrifice required in parenting follows Jesus' example at the Last Supper when he washes the feet of his followers and says that we must live in loving service to others.

> The sacrifice required in parenting follows Jesus' example at the Last Supper when he washes the feet of his followers and says that we must live in loving service to others.

Trust me when I share that Kristi and I fall short frequently in our parenting. We miss opportunities. We overreact. I fail to be as generous as I could be. Kristi might forget to play the long game with the boys at times. I share this to help you avoid the *perfectionism* trap. You fall short, too. And that's okay. Saint Teresa of Calcutta once said, "God does not require that we be successful, only that we be faithful."

Parenting is not about doing everything right all the time. It is about steadfast love. And yes, hopefully succeeding a lot more than we fail...because what we have been called to is really, *really* important. With God's help, our hearts can grow to meet our role and responsibilities.

How do see your parenting role?
As beautiful...impactful...sacrificial...exhausting?

Incalculable Love

YOU KNOW HOW YOU LOOK UPON YOUR CHILD? WITH A LOVE BIGGER THAN YOU THOUGHT POSSIBLE. I'm convinced that's how God looks upon us. Parenting is a window into the mind...and heart...of our God! And it's how parents give children their first inkling of who God is and what unconditional love feels like.

I'll always remember an ordinary midwinter evening. Kristi was putting our toddler, Matthew, to bed. Four-year-old Danny was already in his PJs but hanging out near the kitchen, where I was cleaning up. A folk song called "Daddy's Chair" (about a father who died) was playing, and I felt a pull on my heart. Now, I pride myself on being "tough dad" and saying "no" a lot to the boys. Usually, they have to earn their treats. But this time I called Dan into the kitchen and broke off and shared a part of the candy cane I was about to have.

Dan looked up and asked, "What's this for, Dad?" And I said, "Just because." He put it in his mouth, smiled at me and trotted up the stairs. My heart nearly burst with joy and love just then. Be attentive to these kinds of moments. Look for opportunities to give and receive extraordinary grace in the most ordinary of living. These moments abound and God is there!

Is there anything your children can do to make you stop loving them? Of course not. And so it is with our God.

That evening I was able to reveal for my boy the heart of God, who loves us *just because*. And Dan got a taste of this ultimate truth. We are loved not because of our externals or achievements. We are loved and fed by Jesus simply because we are each God's beloved one, in whom the divine image is reflected.

Is there anything your children can do to make you stop loving them? Of course not. And so it is with our God. God's faithfulness and the love I have for my family combine to inspire a deepening posture of gratitude. I have been given so much!

Parenting is the closest we'll come in this life to seeing the world and loving people as God does. It is a holy role, a calling, a *vocation*! To be our best in this calling, we must lean on God's grace for strength and sustenance. And channel, as much as possible, God's full and perfect love for us, embodied in Jesus, into our children and into the world.

Spend some time observing your children
and reflecting on your love for them.
Ponder how God's love for you
is even greater.

The Mass

Word and Sacrament Celebrated

JESUS IS THE GREAT GIFT FROM GOD, THE FATHER. The Eucharist is Jesus' great gift of himself. And the Mass is where the Eucharist becomes available to us. Let us begin our journey into the mystery of divine love for us and our children, revealed in Jesus and the Eucharist.

The Gospel of Luke was written about 80 AD. Many Scripture scholars consider it to be the most refined of the four Gospel accounts. It portrays Jesus' ministry as primarily being about two things: *healing* and *feeding*.

The Road to Emmaus (Luke 24:13–35) is a rich, multilay-ered narrative of Jesus coming upon and walking with two despondent disciples who are leaving Jerusalem after the exe-cution of their Lord. (Consider reading it right now.) In the story, Jesus walks with them, unrecognized. Then light begins to overtake their darkness as Jesus explains the meaning of the Scriptures relating to him.

When they reach their destination for the evening, the dis-ciples beg him to stay. Jesus takes bread, blesses it, breaks it, and gives it to them to eat. (Luke uses this fourfold formula to convey, as in the Last Supper, that this meal *is* Eucharist.) Simultaneously, they recognize Jesus and he vanishes from their midst. And they feel *compelled* to return to Jerusalem immediately to share the uncontainable good news that Jesus is alive and "how he was made known to them in the breaking of the bread" (Luke 24:35).

There is much to unpack here. Jesus wants to accompany us in our struggles and despair. Encountering Jesus is good news that can't wait until morning. It reorients our lives, opening us to new ways of seeing and living.

Luke was capturing the theological consciousness of first-century Christians here. *Where was Jesus to be found forty years after his life and ministry?* In the assembly of his disciples as they proclaim the Scriptures (as was the Jewish worship custom) and gather around the table to share in the "breaking of the bread" (the new element brought into Christian worship).

What we do today at Mass has its most basic structure reflected in this Easter Day story. The first half of Mass is largely about proclaiming and reflecting upon the Scriptures. This is called the *Liturgy of the Word*. Then, in the *Liturgy of the Eucharist*, the gathered community joins in the prayer of the presiding priest and the Eucharist becomes real on the altar through the power of the Holy Spirit.

An important historical-theological point is found here and revealed elsewhere in the New Testament and in the early Church. Mass is not the concoction of someone's medieval imagination. The liturgy has its origins in Jewish worship and in the Last Supper. The earliest Christians were people of Scripture and Sacrament. And so are we.

What's good news in your life that you love to share with your children? With others?

Real Presence

What and Why

Catholic faith believes in the "Real Presence" of Jesus in the Sacrament of the Eucharist. This means that what we receive and consume at Communion time *is* Jesus. Not in a way that the Romans thought was cannibalistic, but in a mystical and yet literal way. Jesus, Body and Blood, soul and divinity, is present and made available to us in the Eucharist.

This ought to feel outrageous. It is! And yet, Catholic faith is unwavering in this conviction...and has been for 2,000 years. The Eucharist is at the epicenter of God's saving action in human history and represents the culmination of the Gospel ("good news") Jesus came to reveal and embody. It is the most personal and intimate means by which we are able to access Jesus, to enter into physical-spiritual communion with him. The Eucharist is our great inheritance and sacramental entryway into the heart of God.

Why do Catholics believe that the bread and wine brought forth to the altar at Mass are transubstantiated (literally, the substance crosses over) into the Body and Blood of Jesus? Two basic reasons:

1. *Jesus said it*: The Gospels of Matthew, Mark, and Luke similarly narrate the Last Supper, which occurred on the night before Jesus suffered and died on Good Friday. Each of them, along with Saint Paul's First Letter to the Corinthians, attribute to Jesus the words "This is my body" when referring to the bread he prayed over.

> Then he took the bread, said the blessing, broke it, and gave it to them, saying, "This is my body, which will be given for you; do this in memory of me." LUKE 22:19

In this climactic moment of Jesus' life and ministry, as he is about to be arrested, sentenced, tortured, and publicly executed, Catholics take Jesus at his word. Jesus said it and he did it with great intentionality, providing a way for him to remain present to his disciples (then, now, and always).

2. *The early disciples believed it:* We find in the New Testament (the Acts of the Apostles and the Letters of Saint Paul) that the first disciples shared in the eucharistic meal as Jesus had asked them to do. There is also lots of evidence in the writing of the early Church Fathers (Saint Irenaeus, Saint Cyprian, Saint Augustine, and many others) of clear belief in the Real Presence of Jesus in the Eucharist from the second century on. As just one example, Saint John Chrysostom wrote, "He gives you Himself, not only to look at, but to touch, and to eat, and to receive within you."

> Catholics at Mass today participate in an unbroken chain of faith and practice going all the way back to the Last Supper.

Catholics at Mass today participate in an unbroken chain of faith and practice going all the way back to the Last Supper. And while some Christian traditions, beginning in the 16th century, backed away from belief in the Real Presence of Jesus in the Eucharist, Orthodox and Anglican (Episcopalian) churches retain this ancient core precept of Christianity. (Lutherans also believe in Real Presence, with a nuance.)

Real Presence theology means that an incredible miracle is happening right before our eyes at every Mass. The Holy Spirit descends upon and changes the nature of the bread and wine into the Body and Blood of Jesus. Why can't we perceive it with our senses? How does it happen? While I like being able to figure things out as much as the next person, the power of God is beyond us, and happily so. I'm glad to have a God bigger than myself.

In case you are someone in need of some "sensory" evidence, the history of the Church contains remarkable accounts of eucharistic miracles, many of which have been scientifically verified. Check it out.

How good are you at assenting to realities
beyond your ability to fully comprehend?

Life as Journey

"THE BEAUTY IS IN THE WALKING. WE ARE BETRAYED BY DESTINATIONS."

As a young man, I came to appreciate this line from the Welsh poet, Gwyn Thomas. I started seeing my life in terms of *journey*. Meaning-filled, beautiful, and often challenging journey.

In my 30s, I chose to take a road trip journey in my Honda Civic. Having quit my job and sold my home, I went off on an adventure without a hard-and-fast plan. It was scary. At first, I wanted to turn back and reclaim the nice, familiar life I had enjoyed. But it felt like God was beckoning me toward something.

Many blessings came to me on that six-month drive around western North America. I learned that there is less to fear out there than I thought. That going off the grid was exhilarating. That solitude opened me to interior growth.

I loved being unplugged and free. But I also felt the pull to reconnect somehow. And so, as a Catholic, I would find my way to Mass. *Every* weekend...except the time I camped in Death Valley. No Eucharist there. Poetic justice, one might say.

Sometimes in suburban churches, sometimes in national-al parks, in cathedrals and small towns, I returned home. I shared a part of my Sabbath with people who were my brothers and sisters in Christ, though I didn't know their names. I heard the same Scriptures and fed on the same sacramental meal my family and friends were having back home.

Catholic means *universal*. I experienced this in a visceral way while exploring the continent and finding myself. Mass was my Sunday home-visit and my fueling station. I was then ready to take on the adventures and challenges that were surely awaiting me around the next bend.

They say to give your kids roots and wings. My parents and the eucharistic faith they instilled in me gave me both.

*You are on a journey. Chart your past
and consider what lies ahead.*

Family Road Trip

EVEN WITH YOUNG CHILDREN, KRISTI AND I HAVE BEEN BRAVE
(OR FOOLISH) ENOUGH TO ALREADY HAVE TAKEN SOME VERY
LONG CAR TRIPS. All in all, they've been great...the requisite
spit-up and other such "complications" notwithstanding.

Back when I worked in a Catholic parish, I enjoyed helping the children preparing for First Communion. Each year I
would ask them if they had ever taken a long car trip. Hands
would go up and destinations from coast to coast were named.
Once I even got "Hawaii"!

Did you stop along the way or go straight through? They shared
about all the stops: meals, bathroom, gas, sleep, roadside attrac-

tions. *What would have happened without the stops?* We talked about all the bad things that might result. Hunger. Increasing jabs and yelps in the backseat. Even running out of gas! And then I tried to help them see that Jesus offers us Mass as a chance to stop all the going and doing, to rest, reset, and be filled with graces and blessings. God doesn't want our gas gauge to hit "E."

Life is a dynamic journey. God wants to re-create us in his love continually. Did you ever think of Mass in terms of "recreation"? Maybe we should. In our multitasking and oh-so-demanding world (especially in raising a family), maybe we need to find ways to slow down and enter into a different kind of space. Perhaps we can reframe Catholic Sunday worship as part of a healthier lifestyle, where we stop with our family and rest in God.

Jesus wants to accompany us, as he did with the disciples on the Road to Emmaus. He invites us into a relationship of lifelong intimacy as we navigate our lives. He wants to be our nourishment, our life source. Jesus died on the Cross to make this possible, and the Eucharist is his primary means of refueling us.

As parents you pour yourself out continually. And God knows that you can't only give and give and sustain well-being. Are you open to receiving from Jesus?

Jesus in Our Midst

A STUDENT ONCE ASKED ME WHY HE COULDN'T JUST GO OUT INTO THE WOODS ON SUNDAY AND EXPERIENCE JESUS BY READING THE BIBLE. Happily, I was quick on my feet and said that he should totally do that...either before or after going to Mass.

Of course, we are able to experience the presence of Jesus, Son of God and our Savior, outside of Mass. Jesus is the Second Person of the Trinity. He is God. So, we can connect with him in prayer anytime, anywhere. And Jesus is the

Word-made-flesh, God incarnate. So, we can encounter him in a very real way when we read Scripture. These are both great ways to invite Jesus in.

At the Liturgy of the Eucharist, however, we have a powerful, multifaceted experience of Jesus Christ that is unlike anything else. In fact, as the Second Vatican Council (1962–65) taught, four manifestations of our Lord occur in every Mass.

1. Jesus is present in the Word of God proclaimed.

2. Jesus is present in the *assembly*—the people gathered who comprise the body of Christ, as Saint Paul calls the baptized.

3. Jesus is present in the presiding priest who, during the Eucharistic Prayer, acts in the person of Christ.

4. Jesus is present in the Sacrament of the Eucharist made real on the altar and shared with us during the Communion Rite.

As I like to say, that's a lot of Jesus! Nowhere else does Jesus become so available to us and our children. Even if Mass might sometimes feel routine or even boring, there is our saving Lord abundantly present in our midst, seeking to engage with us and transform us, personally and communally.

Transformed for Mission

WHEN RECEIVING THE EUCHARIST, CATHOLICS RESPOND TO "THE BODY OF CHRIST" BY SAYING, "AMEN." Amen means "so be it." When we say, "Amen," we are affirming what is being proposed. We are saying "yes." Catholics, unfortunately, often receive the Eucharist without being fully conscious of the significance of this.

Our "Amen" should be about two things: 1) Yes, I believe that what I'm receiving is the transubstantiated Body and Blood of Christ Jesus. And, just as importantly, 2) Yes, I am willing to be(come) what I eat. I am willing to be the presence of Jesus in the world, to bring his joy and forgiveness, his tenderness and strength to those I encounter each day.

Seeing ourselves as living, breathing tabernacles who carry Jesus in us may be just as hard as believing in the Real Presence teaching. The first "yes" is an act of faith. The second is a commitment to action.

Just before ascending into heaven, Jesus told his followers to bring the good news of the Father's saving love to all corners of the planet. He was entrusting to them (and us!) his mission. And so, Jesus provides all that we need to be his disciples-on-mission: his teaching and miracles, his friendship and mercy, his very life surrendered on the Cross. And, on the night before he died, his Body and Blood as sacred food to nourish us.

Jesus died and rose to unleash the full power of God to transform *everything*. The Eucharist must be understood as more than simply a personal gift to be squirreled away like some spiritual acorn. It is a sacrament, an instrument of grace, to bless and transform each of us. *And* it is an inheritance to be shared out in who we are and how we live.

On our own, perhaps we can do a lot of good. But on our own, we have little hope of bringing the full measure of God's grace to our family, friends, neighbors, and coworkers. If we feed on Christ Jesus (in Word, in Sacrament, and in community), God can slowly but surely mold us into the Christlike persons we are called to be and *want* to be for our children and others. And then we have a real chance, locally and globally, to confront evil, offer hope to the hopeless, and sow seeds of justice, peace, and love.

Saint Augustine describes what each Communion Rite should be for us: "Believe what you see, see what you believe, and become what you are: the Body of Christ." When we receive the Sacrament of the Eucharist at Mass, we're making a commitment to love as we have been loved; to feed others as we are fed. With our "Amen" we are accepting Jesus' invitation to go on mission with him! And that mission starts in our own home!

The term "Mass" comes from the Latin word *missa* or mission. At the end of each Mass, the priest (or deacon) commissions us and sends us forth to be, as Saint Teresa of Avila exhorts, the hands and feet and eyes of Jesus for others. Christian disciples are not supposed to hide from the world but engage it. We leave well resourced, for we bring the Risen Christ with us.

How do you feel about saying **yes** *to the mission of Jesus?*

The Human Heart

WHAT DO YOU HUNGER FOR? Once upon a time, I was a sucker for french fries. I still like them but I'm actually more into salads as an adult. My arteries are appreciative.

Food is a part of my question. But of course, I'm asking about more than food. What do you long for? What do you consume to satisfy the hungers of your heart?

I remember one night watching a show about a spend-aholic wife and mom. A counselor was brought in to explore the roots of her behavior and surmised that something at her core was hollow. She was trying to fill that aching interior space with experiences and with stuff.

There are a lot of things we can reach for in our world today that offer us the promise of satisfaction. It can be almost anything...food, alcohol and drugs, experiences, status, things. For a while, these choices can fill our empty space. But the satisfaction doesn't last for all that long. And so, just like with hi-carb treats, we soon end up hungry again and caught in an unhealthy cycle of chasing the high.

My favorite Old Testament story is in the First Book of Kings. Early in the account (1 Kings 19:3–13), the prophet Elijah is in a spiritual-emotional place of desolation and goes out into the desert. He finds a tree under which he hopes to die. An angel (God's agent) comes twice to wake him and minister to him with food and drink, telling Elijah the second time, "Get up and eat or the journey will be too much for you!"

I've been there, locked in a space of torment and despair. Perhaps you have, too. It's dark there. No hope and very scary...or very sad. This story reveals the tender heart of the Father for us, for *each* of us, especially in our darkest times and deepest struggles. And it is a foreshadowing of Jesus, God-made-Flesh, whose entire life is a sacramental outreach to embrace, uplift, and rescue us.

Jesus, at the climactic moment of his life and ministry to humanity, feeds us in an ultimate way. Not with wine at the wedding in Cana. Not with a multiplication of loaves and

fishes. The food and drink Jesus most desires us to feed on...
to feast on...is *himself*.

The Last Supper and the Cross (bound intrinsically together) provide the punchline in the greatest love story ever told. It
is about divine love for us and our family that is unledition-
al, that transcends the calculating limits of logic. It is about a
personal God who empties himself completely in Jesus and is
crazy in love with us. (Read the story
of the Prodigal Son at Luke 15:11–32 if
you doubt this.)

There is a second part to Elijah's
story. God commands Elijah to ascend
a mountain and wait for God to reveal
himself. Wind, earthquake, and fire
each come to the mountain, but none
contains God. No, God is not in the
powerful and the showy. Rather, God

> The Last Supper and the Cross (bound intrinsically together) provide the punchline in the greatest love story ever told.

comes as a small, soft sound. And Elijah steps forward to
engage the whisper.

There is a danger that comes with parenting. It can be
almost all-consuming, on top of our many other responsibilities. If our lives are too busy, too noisy, we run the risk of
missing the gentle voice and the message offered to each of
us. That would be a terrible shame, for it is a message of deep,
transforming love for *you*.

Jesus Christ embodies this divine love, literally. His teachings, his miracles, and his sacrificial action on the Cross reveal a God who has gone before us in suffering and knows our pain and grief. And the Eucharist is his ultimate gift, representing Jesus and his desire for communion with us.

What do you hunger for?

Saint Teresa of Calcutta, who dedicated her life to the poorest of India, once said of Western societies, "Everywhere today hunger is not only for a piece of bread, but hunger for God, hunger for love."

Maybe the deeper question for each of us is,
*"**Whom** do you hunger for?"*

Why Bother

COMMITMENT IS HARD. Showing up and giving our best each day, each moment, be it at work or home, is really hard. It is much easier to phone it in when we don't feel like showing up. And if we don't radically lean on God to sustain us, we will fall short of our aspiration too often. Heck, I fall short even *with* a deep connectedness to Jesus and his Church.

There are times I don't feel like going to church. I bet most everyone experiences this. Folks might want to sleep in or watch the pregame show or just not have to deal with people. I totally get it.

But I'll let you in on another secret. And it is the God's honest truth. I have never left Mass...*never*...saying, "That was a mistake. Wish I hadn't done that." Even when the liturgy wasn't particularly inspiring. I find that utterly amazing. And telling.

One of the many great things about the Catholic faith is that it calls me to a consciousness bigger than just my own. It challenges me to live into a spirit of generosity. Catholic faith opens me to God's grace, which can heal my brokenness and empower me to love beyond my natural capacity. My potential is not limited by my inclinations. How hopeful is that!

As Catholics, we ground our faith life in our identity as "baptized." It all goes back to that sacramental action that our parents likely took on our behalf. Baptism conveys upon us a dignity; it disposes us to grace and orients us to the person of Jesus and a life of discipleship. Make no mistake: to be baptized is a huge deal!

With God's help, on the Sundays I feel like it and on the Sundays I don't, I go to Mass. It is a commitment to live as a baptized member in the body of Christ. I don't weigh factors. There's no deliberation. I just go, with my wife and kids. I am in with both feet, comparable to the commitment I hold in being a husband and father.

Of course, having children makes the whole Mass process more challenging. Herding the cats before Mass is not much fun. (Keep in mind that we can offer up any and all of our sacrifices to God, who gladly receives them as blessings that return to us and others.) But it is also all the more meaningful, because attending Mass is now also about the boys and their spiritual-moral development.

Like you, I'm all in for giving them what is good, whatever it takes. For Kristi and me, God has to come first. Anywhere else in the pecking order just makes no sense.

These are the three core reasons for my commitment to Catholic Mass (in addition to now modeling *eucharistic faith* for my children):

1. *I go to Mass for God.* God is good and deserving of all my love. I am a beloved creature of the Creator. I need to worship! Everything I have is gift. And I must praise and thank God for all of it: every moment, every breath. To worship in gratitude and awe is the most authentically human action I can take in this life. (*Eucharist* is actually a Greek early Christian word meaning "thanksgiving.")

2. *I go for me.* I am a screw-up. Just like the apostles, I get it wrong a lot. I cannot be the man and father I want to be without grace. The eucharistic liturgy nourishes me with God's Word, with the Bread of Life, and with parish community for the joys and challenges, setbacks and possibilities that await.

3. *I go for you.* I may not know the names of the people around me. And yet, I attend Mass for them, for *you.* Whether I'm at my home parish or traveling, those worshiping with me are my brothers and sisters in Jesus. We are baptized members of the one body of Christ, the Church. Baptism calls on me to stand with my kin, to pray with them, to pray for them. And they have come to stand with me. I am not alone! Together, we are community...Christian community. That is beautiful. That is powerful.

Acclaimed Catholic writer, Flannery O'Connor, who endured great challenge in her short life, wrote, "You will have found Christ when you are concerned with other people's sufferings and not your own." Catholic worship is about accessing the perfect sacrifice of Jesus on Calvary and joining in solidarity with one another's crosses. Dying and rising is what we ritually celebrate.

Mass is not meant to be *fun.* Liturgy is not *entertainment.* It is actually so very much more.

What has been your
perception of Mass?

Leaning into *More*

MANY ADULTS (CATHOLIC OR NOT) HAVE A COMPLICATED, EVEN CONTENTIOUS RELATIONSHIP WITH CATHOLICISM; they may feel drawn to aspects of the faith but have doubts and disagreements, too. Being a parent can provide us with the opportunity and motivation to re-engage and to give faith and the faith community another look.

What I can share is that Catholic faith is the greatest gift my parents gave me. I grew up in a strong parish community, holding a broad and hopeful worldview and living a lifestyle filled with love, values, and a sense of purpose. My Catholic faith and love for Jesus (in Scripture and Eucharist) have guided me through the hardest times of my life.

Kristi and I want this above all else for our children: something bigger than just ourselves and the values of merely this time and place. We want their hearts set on fire and their eye level raised to heaven. We want them to become the heroic, amazing people they were made to be!

When I hold parent sessions, those gathered share what they want for their children: safety, health, success, and, most of all, happiness. Of course. Parents are dedicated to giving to their children the best that life has to offer. Remember, it's how parents are wired by God...to embody and convey divine love.

Happiness is a funny thing, though. It comes and goes thanks to all sorts of variables. Catholic faith offers the possibility of something deeper and more sustained than happiness. The Gospel of Jesus Christ makes possible in us something that the world cannot give: *joy*.

If happiness is a state of mind, joy is a state of grace. It is a supernatural gift that allows us to endure and rise above the hard stuff: heartbreak, financial struggles, a tough health diagnosis, or the passing of a loved one. In the end, the demonstrated power of God in Jesus Christ to roll away the stone is greater than any of this. Sin and death have no real power over us anymore!

The fourteenth-century mystic Julian of Norwich framed Christian understanding in stark, poetic terms: "All shall be well, and all shall be well and all manner of thing shall be well." As they begin their grace-filled and daunting life journey, what greater knowledge can we teach our children? What deeper confidence can we instill?

Catholic sacraments are not magic. But they are *effective*. Baptism powerfully signifies the new context in which the baptized Christian lives: "We were indeed buried with him through baptism into death, so that, just as Christ was raised from the dead by the glory of the Father, we too might live in newness of life" (Romans 6:4). The implication is as fresh and relevant for you (as a baptized person) as it is for your child. But grace builds upon nature, and God's invitation requires a response.

So, too, with the Eucharist: "Jesus said to them, 'I am the bread of life; whoever comes to me will never hunger, and whoever believes in me will never thirst'" (John 6:35). Jesus wants to be our nourishment. As a mother nurses her child, so God pours out life-giving grace to us in Baptism and in Eucharist. Jesus and the sacraments of the Church are signs of God's active love for you and for your family.

What does the prospect of being joyful do to your heart?

Bringing It Home
Catholic Practicalities

ROBERT COLES, A HARVARD PROFESSOR, PSYCHIATRIST, AND AUTHOR, DISCOVERED IN HIS RESEARCH THAT CHILDREN HAVE AN INNATE SENSE OF GOD AND TRANSCENDENCE. The implication is that parents are not responsible for creating faith in their children so much as cultivating that which God has planted in our nature.

Sofia Cavalletti, co-founder of Catechesis of the Good Shepherd, a Montessori-based approach to Catholic religious education, wrote of the existential need children have to experience God's love personally and be provided with specific religious formation that mediates the experience and frames its meaning.

Maria Montessori herself spoke, in a 1927 interview, about the importance of formal, experiential Catholic catechesis for children: "The child must learn how to make the Sign of the Cross...be taught the actions of the Mass...and, in general, how to participate in the liturgical ceremonies of the Church."

There is no time like today to embrace the opportunity to explore God's love with your children. And try not to lament any failings to date. "This is the day the Lord has made; let us rejoice in it and be glad" (Psalm 118:24). Whether your child is a toddler or an adolescent, you have a central role to play in their faith development *now*.

Consider three areas of focus for nurturing their spiritual and religious formation:

1) Talk *faith* as a family, giving what you have and seeking to grow in faith understanding yourself.

2) Provide experiences of prayer and faith ritual to create a culture of Catholic practice in your home. Blessing your children, for example. Experiencing meals together as a sacred time of family bonding and care. And more.

3) Be a family that serves others—not just to be nice or good, but in the name of Christ Jesus, our Savior. Remember, actions speak louder than words, especially with young people.

This little book is very limited in its scope. There are lots of amazing Catholic resources to deepen adult and family faith—spiritually, biblically, and theologically. Become a life-long learner! It will bless you!

Regarding online resources, understand that not all are created equal out there. Connect with your Catholic parish for guidance and support as you and your family seek to grow in faith.

Here are just a couple of suggestions for enriching eucharistic and family faith:

WhyMass.org
CatholicFamilyFaith.org

I've written two short books about Eucharist and the Mass. *Group Reading Guide: Eucharist* is a spiritual reflection on the parts of the Mass; *How to Talk to Children about the Mass* is meant to help parents in their formative role. Perhaps they could help to further develop and deepen your eucharistic faith and practice. (Both are from Twenty-Third Publications, which has many other great Catholic resources.)

If you truly want faith for your children, you'll want to start by becoming more prayerful and living more reflectively. Remember: *You can't give what you don't have.* Strive to create moments of quiet contemplation, sometimes perhaps before the Blessed Sacrament, the Real Presence of Jesus in every Catholic church's tabernacle.

God wants a relationship of ongoing dialogue with us. Pray regularly for your children and for yourself. But try to listen at least as much as you talk. And ask your children to pray for you. They will.

I hope you are excited at the prospect of a path of spiritual discovery and growth awaiting you. The journey for me has been amazing and it is only getting richer. I can attest from very real, personal experience that God's heart for each of us is patient, merciful and oh-so deep. There is no joy greater than living into the mystery that Jesus is risen and has defeated death...*for love of us.*

This divine, unconditional love warrants a personal response from each of us. For me, it is to spend the rest of my life surrendering to it, conforming to it, and sharing it with others. *Beginning* with my family.

How do you want to respond to
God's love revealed in Jesus?

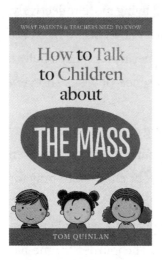